MW01223475

BOOK ANALYSIS

Written by Mélanie Ackerman
Translated by Ciaran Traynor

Three Strong Women

by Marie NDiaye

Bright
≡Summaries.com

MARIE NDIAYE

FRENCH NOVELIST, DRAMATIST
AND SHORT STORY WRITER

- **Born in 1967 in Pithiviers, France.**
- **Notable works:**
  - *La femme changée en bûche* ("Woman into Log", 1989), novel
  - *Rosie Carpie* (2001), novel
  - *Three Strong Women* (2009), novel

Marie NDiaye was born in 1967 and is a novelist, dramatist and short story writer. She has written several dozen works, among which are 12 novels, including *Rosie Carpie* and *Three Strong Women*, which were awarded the Prix Femina and Prix Goncourt respectively.

Although born to a French mother and a Senegalese father, NDiaye was brought up in France and has only been to Africa once, in the 1980s. Her work is sometimes linked to the *négritude* movement developed by franco-phone African writers and thinkers due to her

Senegalese origins, but NDiaye does not claim to belong to any literary movement.

THREE STRONG WOMEN

FEMALE HEROISM

- **Genre**: novel
- **Reference edition**: NDiaye, M. (2012) Three Strong Women. Trans. Fletcher, J. London: MacLehose Press.
- **1st edition**: 2009
- **Themes**: women, rebellion, family, Senegal, cowardice, courage

Three Strong Women (2009) is the work which made NDiaye famous – there is a reason the book won the Prix Goncourt. Three different, apparently unrelated stories unfold in the novel; all that links them is the fact that they all involve women. Nevertheless, a common theme emerges: the difficulties faced by modern women. In all three of the texts, it is a man's mediocrity which reveals the strength of each of these women. Moreover, a secondary character links one story to the next.

SUMMARY

THE FIRST STORY

Norah has really made it in life: she is a lawyer and lives with her partner Jakob, her daughter and Jakob's son. The young woman goes to visit her father after receiving a call from him. Her partner and children surprise her by joining her later on.

When she arrives, she does not recognise this stranger who does not care about his appearance or good manners, things which her father placed great value upon. Norah spent little time with her father: she grew up with her mother and her sister after he took away her brother Sony to Africa, where he made his fortune and pretended to be a tough guy. Now, Norah finds him alone in an empty house. However, she discovers two little girls locked in a room, who she assumes are her father's children. Her father, on the other hand, lives in the tree in front of the house. Norah also finds out that her brother is in prison for killing his stepmother, his father's latest wife with whom he was having an affair.

When her brother confesses that the culprit in the murder case is actually their father, the young woman agrees to fight his case. He also admits that the twins that Norah saw are actually his children, born out of his relationship with his stepmother. After speaking to her father, Norah discovers that he blames his wife, not Sony, which highlights how backward he truly is: he clearly believes women are always guilty.

THE SECOND STORY

Fanta left her home country of Senegal to go to France with her husband, Rudy Descas, after an incident with some teenagers in Dakar. However, Rudy actually lied to her: it was he who attacked the teenagers, not the other way around as he claimed. Ever since, their life has continued to grow more and more difficult: Fanta has not managed to get a job as a teacher and her husband, who had promised her a wonderful life, has not been able to keep his promises. They have to make do with his unexciting job as a kitchen salesman, which Rudy only managed to get thanks to his mother's intervention with his boss, Manille, who also had an affair with Fanta.

Painfully aware of his mediocrity, Rudy realises that Fanta no longer loves him and sinks into despair. Eaten away by the past, he constantly thinks about the man he used to be before he returned to France. On his way to work, he remembers the fight he had with his wife that morning. In a fit of rage, he told her "you can go back where you came from".

Feeling guilty, afraid and terrified that his wife will leave him, Rudy tries to call Fanta. However, once he reaches her, she plays coy. After a bit of thinking, he realises that what he said to Fanta could be taken to mean "go back to Manille".

He then finds out that his mother has dropped by at his work to leave some leaflets about the existence of angels. The first copy has been scribbled on, which angers Rudy, as he cannot bear the idea of someone making fun of his mother's beliefs. Manille says it was not him, claiming that he could never do that to Rudy's mother: when he was little, he used to spend every Wednesday afternoon at her house. When he learns this, Rudy's jealousy grows even greater, because his mother had never told him it was his boss that she used to invite over.

On the way to meet an unhappy client, a buzzard hits his car and injures Rudy's head. When he meets the client, the salesman realises that he has made a serious mistake in the kitchen and knows that he is going to be fired. On the journey back, he cannot help himself from driving through the area where a certain sculptor lives. The man had once made a sculpture with an uncanny similarity to Rudy. When he sees his house, Rudy suddenly grows jealous of this "pathetic artist". He considers killing him, which reminds him of his own father, who murdered his partner.

When he goes to pick up his son Djibril, he has another encounter with the buzzard, which has already hit him several times. The atmosphere between father and son is tense. The little boy is behaving like Fanta.

When he goes to drop Djibril off at his grandmother's house, he finds a neighbourhood boy who has come for a snack. Rudy realises that his mother thinks that the boy is an angel. Seeing her draw a picture of the child, a wave of repulsion washes over him, and he has the feeling that he is seeing his mother's true face for the very first time. As he is leaving the house, he runs over a bird. However, he pays this no mind: he is in a good mood and is looking forward to going home. Fanta's neighbour sees him and is amazed at how happy he seems. The two neighbours say hello to each other for the first time ever.

THE THIRD STORY

When her husband died, Khady Demba had no-one to turn to but her in-laws. They look down on her, and so she puts all her energy into household tasks and slowly withdraws into herself. When her in-laws tell her that she has to leave, she is overcome with terror. They tell her about Fanta, a cousin living in France, but she does not listen to them.

Khady is taken to a busy courtyard by a man, who forces her to walk, and then put in a car. During the journey she sees several crows, which she associates with the children she never had. Without knowing where she is being taken, she is "still happy to utter her name silently and to feel it in such harmony with the precise, satisfying image she had of her own features". During the night, they get into a leaking boat. However, Khady manages to escape and runs to the beach, where she falls asleep.

When she wakes up, a young man called Lamine is watching her. They introduce themselves. Over the next few days, they slowly grow closer as they each realise that they both want to go to Europe. Khady learns a lot from him, because all she knows about life comes from her own experiences. Nobody has ever looked after her like this.

One morning, they board a truck heading for Europe, but they are quickly stopped. Khady is then forced to sell her body to get by. In spite of the humiliation, she keeps telling herself that she is "Khady Demba in all her singularity", until she discovers that Lamine has betrayed her and gone off with all her hard-earned money. When he reaches Europe, he thinks about "the girl" every payday, hoping that she will find it in herself to forgive him.

Some time later, Khady finds herself in a camp

where everyone is working on building a ladder. She decides to join in. One night, they all take their ladders to the wall which separates them from Europe. Khady tries to ignore her wounds and gives it everything she has. In spite of her best efforts, one moment of weakness is all it takes for her to tumble to the ground. As she lies there, she spots a bird, and suddenly has the strangest feeling that she is looking at herself.

CHARACTER STUDY

THE FIRST STORY

Norah

Norah is the protagonist of the first story. She is a modern young mother who lives in Paris with her daughter, her partner and his son. She is a symbol of success, as well as logic and morality.

Abandoned and scorned by her father while she was still a child, she has still managed to become a brilliant lawyer. In the story, she ends up helping and taking pity on her father.

Norah's father

Norah's father has had several wives and children. After years of prosperity, he finds himself penniless and alone, which is why he calls Norah for help. When she arrives, she sees how far her father has fallen: he can now do nothing but watch as the time goes by and people slowly drift away from him. He is no longer the tyrant that she once knew, but just a broken man living in the flame tree in front of his house.

Sony

Norah's brother Sony is their father's only son. He was taken away as a boy to live in his country of origin. He represented the change and lineage of his family, but the murder of his mother-in-law changed everything. Now locked up in prison, he wins the support of his sister when she discovers that he is not guilty of the charges brought against him.

Jakob

Norah's partner Jakob is the very opposite of logical, representing both what Norah is looking for in life and what she would like to avoid. She tries to protect herself from surges of tenderness and any other feeling that could make her feel dependent on his love. For this reason, she swings between loving him and hating him.

THE SECOND STORY

Fanta

Fanta, the second strong woman of the story, is Rudy's wife. Unlike in the first story, Fanta is not the focus of the narration. Nevertheless, her presence can be felt throughout the tale, as she seems to be breaking up with her disillusioned husband. She was a teacher in Africa and decided to leave her country to go to France with her husband. However, he and the life he offers her bring her nothing but disappointment. As Rudy continues to make things worse for himself, she faces up to him and acts indifferently. She is a strong woman who eventually appears, to a certain extent, happy.

Rudy Descas

At first glance, Rudy has everything he needs to be happy. However, his apparent success hides a weary man who knows that his life is going downhill. He seems to enjoy being so mediocre that others move away from him.

Manille

Rudy's boss is everything that he is not: he is a man who has succeeded in life and takes pleasure in his work. This is perhaps why Fanta falls for him.

Rudy's mother

Rudy's mother is convinced that angels exist and tries to share this belief with others. Rudy depends on her a lot and she plays a major part in his life. However, in the end Rudy discovers his mother's true nature and returns to Fanta.

THE THIRD STORY

Khady Demba

Khady Demba is a young African woman who has no choice but to go to live with her in-laws after the death of her husband. They scorn her, exploit her and eventually kick her out, leaving her penniless and alone. For her, Europe is the land of freedom. During her journey, she meets Lamine, who betrays her. She suffers all kinds of pain and humiliation, but she manages to convince herself that she is unique. She holds onto her motto until the very end: "Me, Khady Demba."

Lamine

Khady does not meet Lamine until later on in the story. The two quickly grow close as they realise that they share the same goal. They leave for Europe together, but Lamine betrays her. While she is forced to sell her body to make ends meet, he steals the money she has managed to earn and leaves for Europe. He eventually gets there, thanks to the girl that he left behind on the way.

ANALYSIS

A NOVEL OR A COLLECTION OF SHORT STORIES?

Three Strong Women is a work made up of three stories. As a result, it could be considered a collection of short stories.

According to the Collins English dictionary, a short story is "a prose narrative of shorter length than the novel", while a novel is "an extended work in prose". However, these two definitions do not specify what "of shorter length" or "extended" actually mean. Nevertheless, it is difficult to say that *Three Strong Women* is a collection of short stories, since they are all relatively long in their own right.

There is another reason that *Three Strong Women* could be considered a novel: the three stories are linked to one another, albeit tenuously. There are two types of relationships which bring the three stories together.

- Firstly, similarities can be established between the stories because of their common theme – they all portray women who remain dignified in difficult situations and stand up to men who have lost all sense of pride.
- Secondly, the characters link one story to the next: Khady Demba, the protagonist of the third story, is also the maid of Norah's father, which we discover at the end of the first story and, in the third story, Khady tries to reach Fanta, her cousin living in France who is the protagonist of the second tale.

These different links make us think that the three stories are just different slices of life, like various aspects of one world. On the whole, the novel is therefore a portrayal of contemporary life.

THREE STRONG WOMEN AND THREE COWARDLY MEN

The stories which make up the book show women who are not afraid to stand up for themselves. In this sense, they are the true heroes: they may be "singularly powerless [but] [...] each woman retains a saving core of humanity [...] that's incomprehensible to the fathers, husbands or in-laws who are putting them at risk" (Eberstadt, 2012).

Each of them suffers a life that they have not chosen.

- Norah has to put her family and work to one side to go see her father, even though he abandoned her, her sister and her mother when she was still a child. However, she does much more than that. When she arrives, she discovers that he has lost his fortune and is now living in poverty. Although he disgusts her at first, she eventually takes pity on him. She decides to fight for her brother and grows closer to her father.
- Fanta left her country to stay with her husband and his promises of a good life. Although she was a teacher in Dakar, she cannot get a job in France. The thought of her wasted life haunts her every day. Her husband, on the other hand, wallows in his mediocrity and fails to keep his promises. Yet even faced with this situation, our heroine stays strong.
- Khady Demba is trying to get to Europe. She meets Lamine, who encourages her to prostitute herself before abandoning her and taking

all of her money. Khady bravely overcomes every obstacle that comes her way, reminding herself that she is happy to be herself and that she is unique.

However, highlighting the courage of these women also emphasises the cowardice of the men around them. NDiaye's heroines never let themselves be beaten, no matter how weak the men in their lives are.

- Norah's father used to be a tyrant who ruled over his household with an iron fist. However, when Norah sees him again for the first time in years, she finds him a broken man. His new appearance is a testimony to his life: his wife left him and his son is in prison for a crime that he himself committed.
- Rudy Descas, Fanta's husband, was never able to give her the beautiful house, brand-new car or teaching job that she dreamed of. He is his own worst enemy, as "his arrogance had prevented him noticeably improving his skills".
- Lamine fascinates Khady Demba when they first meet. However, the moment they begin to run out of money, he lets her sell her body, and then he leaves her to her own fate and

makes off with her earnings. Lamine reaches Europe and sometimes thinks of the poor girl that he did not even try to save.

THE BREAKDOWN OF THE FAMILY

In *Three Strong Women*, Marie NDiaye tackles a theme which she has already addressed in her previous books: family. The author not only highlights the gap between the three women and the men in their lives, but also shows how the concept of family is breaking down. In each of these stories, family is hanging together by a thread:

- In the first story, the family is already long gone. When the story begins, Norah's father has already abandoned his wife and daughters to run away with his son. Norah has separated from the father of her child, but she tries to rebuild a family with Jakob, without even knowing if she loves him. In both situations, the father is absent. Paternal absence is a theme that NDiaye also tackled in her first major success: *Rosie Carpe*.
- In the second story, the family seems to be holding on. Nevertheless, the reader learns

about the affair between Fanta and Manille and then discovers the role of Rudy's mother in the breakdown of his marriage and family. Secrets are slowly revealed as the story unfolds, allowing the reader to understand the uneasiness which has taken root between the protagonists.

- Finally, the last story is perhaps also the most touching. No matter how hard she fights, Khady always ends up alone. Abandoned by her parents, a widow after three years of marriage and rejected by her husband's family, the young woman never knows the happiness of a united family.

Heartbreak touches each of these stories. However, none of the heroines ever complain; on the contrary, the tone of the novel helps to reinforce Norah, Fanta and Khady's characters and affirms that they are three strong women.

SENEGAL: THE NOVEL'S BACKGROUND

Marie NDiaye's father is Senegalese, which means that she is of African origin. However, the writer was born in France and refuses to be associated with African literature: she feels more French than African, since she has little knowledge of the land of her father. However, this continent seems to be reflected, perhaps even unconsciously, in her work. The stories in *Three Strong Women* are all linked to Senegal: they either take place there, or the country is a major presence in the tale.

- In the first story, Norah goes to see her father in his native country. Senegal is never explicitly mentioned, but there are several clues which hint that we are in the land of NDiaye's father(Devarrieux, 2009). For example, we are introduced to the village of Dara Salam, the Grand-Yoff area and the newspaper *Le Soleil*, which are all indications that we are in the city of Dakar, the capital of Senegal.
- Although the second story takes place in France, the heroine is African. She left her country for Europe, but she does not find the happiness she is looking for.
- The third story highlights a woman's will to leave Senegal. The story is a testimony of her quest towards Europe and independence, and an account of her fight to get out of her former

life in Senegal.

It should therefore be noted that each of NDiaye's heroines is a woman torn between Senegal and France. Norah, Fanta and Khady have to find their path, their identity and their place between these two nations and continents. The novel therefore looks at "white skin, black skin, and the misunderstandings that they cause"[1] (Devarrieux, 2009). In this way, Marie NDiaye highlights the daily fight of many women in their search for recognition.

---

1. This quotation has been translated by BrightSummaries.com.

FURTHER REFLECTION

SOME QUESTIONS TO THINK ABOUT...

- In your opinion, why did Marie NDiaye not call her book *Three Cowardly Men*?
- Can you see any parallels in these stories with NDiaye's life? Does this make the novel more of an autobiographical story?
- Each part of the novel ends with a contrast. How does this contribute to each story as a whole?
- Details create links between the stories. How can you explain this? In your opinion, why did the author not make these links more obvious?
- Beside the theme of fighting spirit and the character of Khady Demba, what other element establishes a link between the first and last story?
- In your opinion, why does the second story focus on Rudy Descas and not his wife, Fanta?
- What unites NDiaye's three heroines? Develop your answer by referring to the different

stories.

- How do the three heroines differ? Develop your answer by referring to the different stories.
- Is the relationship between Europe (France) and Africa (Senegal) balanced? Explain your answer.
- In your opinion, how does NDiaye add a positive note to these tales? What other elements hint at a better future for these women?
- How would you go about making a cinema adaptation of *Three Strong Women*?

We want to hear from you!
Leave a comment on your online library
and share your favourite books on social media!

FURTHER READING

REFERENCE EDITION

- NDiaye, M. (2012) *Three Strong Women*. Trans. Fletcher, J. London: MacLehose Press.

Although the editor makes every effort to
verify the accuracy of the information published,
BrightSummaries.com accepts no responsibility for
the content of this book.

www.brightsummaries.com

Ebook EAN: 9782808000901

Paperback EAN: 9782808000918

Legal Deposit: D/2017/12603/473

Cover: © Primento

Digital conception by Primento, the digital partner of
publishers.

Made in the USA
Lexington, KY
27 March 2018